MW01145998

When Bad Things Happen

Thoughtful Answers
to Hard Questions

William P. Smith

New
Growth
Press

www.newgrowthpress.com

New Growth Press, Greensboro, NC 27404
Copyright © 2008 by Christian Counseling & Educational Foundation. All rights reserved. Published 2008

Cover Design: The DesignWorks Group, Nate Salciccioli and Jeff Miller, www.thedesignworksgroup.com

Typesetting: Robin Black, www.blackbirdcreative.biz

ISBN-10: 1-934885-41-X
ISBN-13: 978-1-934885-41-3

Library of Congress Cataloging-in-Publication Data

Smith, William P., 1965-
  When bad things happen : thoughtful answers to hard questions / William P. Smith.
      p. cm.
  Includes bibliographical references and index.
  ISBN 978-1-934885-41-3
  1. Suffering—Religious aspects—Christianity. 2. Consolation.
I. Title.
  BT732.7.S64 2008
  231'.8—dc22

                                    2008011943

Printed in Canada
20 19 18 17 16 15 14 13   8 9 10 11 12

"How could a good God have let those things happen to me?" asked Tina. Her experiences growing up with an abusive father stretched into the present, affecting her adult relationships. She had been taught in church that Jesus loves her *and* rules the world, but she couldn't bring those truths together when she thought about her difficult childhood.

So she said to me, "Look, I've known for years that God is in charge of his world, but that leaves me with lots of questions. Why did he give me an abusive father?"

Tina is not the only person to ask, "Why does God let bad things happen to me?" Perhaps you are struggling with this question right now. Because so many people ask this question, you might think there would be one, simple, clear verse in the Bible that would give us *the* answer. Maybe a verse that said, "Because you didn't have enough faith" or "Because God gave people free will." Your friends might have offered you these pat, easy answers, but the answers God gives in the Bible are not easy or pat—they are much more profound and ultimately more satisfying.

God Understands Suffering

The first thing you need to know, even before you consider how God answers your questions about suffering, is that God understands suffering. When your life falls apart—your husband dies, your wife cheats on you, you lose your job, your children reject you, your parents disown you, you become ill, or any other hard thing happens—you want someone in the universe to hear how difficult your struggle is and affirm that you are not crazy or wrong to feel so much anguish.

God does see and hear your suffering. His eyes and ears are peculiarly tuned into it (Genesis 16:7–14; Exodus 2:23–25). We see this most clearly when we consider Jesus. While he lived among us he experienced undeserved deprivation, ridicule, cruelty, and then suffered unimaginable physical and emotional pain as he died on the cross for us.

Because God knows suffering firsthand, we can't say to him, "You don't know what this feels like!"

The Bible tells us that Jesus is a man of sorrows, who is well acquainted with grief (Isaiah 53). He knows more about suffering than anyone else ever has or ever will. And he cares enough to do something about it, though it's often not what you might first expect or want. He comes near to us, and in his presence we are revived to withstand what we're enduring.

Suffering Is an Invitation to Know God

We know from Jesus' life and death that God understands suffering. But why did he allow suffering into the world? Why didn't the all-knowing, all-powerful, good God keep Tina's father from hurting her? If you think about it, you know that's a question that never ends. Why did he allow her dad to be hurt in his own childhood or his parents in theirs? You can legitimately ask that question of every person who has ever lived, going back through history until you arrive at Adam and Eve, the first man and woman. God made them perfect and gave them a perfect relationship in the Garden of Eden, their perfect home. But Satan came into the garden as a snake and tempted them to disobey God. At the moment they disobeyed, sin entered into the world.

Why didn't God intervene when Eve tempted Adam with the forbidden fruit? Why did God allow the snake to deceive Eve? Or even, since we're asking, why allow the serpent to enter the garden? Why, if God is good, wise, just, and strong, didn't he simply destroy Satan? These are not easy questions, and this side of heaven we won't be able to answer them completely. But it is good to wrestle with them, because as we do we will find we are learning to know and love God more deeply.

Let's begin by considering how we get to know one another. One good way is to look at what someone has created. For example, in almost all of my young son's drawings he includes himself and a friend—even if it's his stuffed dog—along with some kind of sports equipment. His drawings give you an idea of how strongly he values relationships and activity. When I look at my son's pictures, I understand him better—what he creates reflects who he is. The same is true of what God created. God made creation to display himself—to show his invisible, eternal power and divine nature by what he has made (Romans 1:18–20).

What does creation tells us about the Creator? We look at beautiful birds, flowers, and sunsets and learn that God loves beauty. We look at the sun, moon, stars, oceans, and mountains and learn how big God is. We see the intricacy of muscles, nerves, tendons, and bone in our hands and know that God is creative and inventive.

We also learn about God from the way he relates to what he created. For instance, what do we learn about God from observing how he handled the time long before human history, when the angels he created rejected his dominion over them? When they rebelled against God, he dismissed them from heaven and sentenced them to be apart from him forever (Matthew 25:41; Jude 6; Revelation 12:7–12).

From God's response to the angels' disobedience, we learn he is holy and expects absolute obedience and conformity to his purposes and plans. We learn that disobeying him produces judgment. We learn he has the power and the will to execute his judgments.

In a creation unmarred by sin, you would not know such terrifying depths of your Maker.

So why go through another episode of rebellion in the Garden of Eden? Because this time we learn something different. Not only is there wrath and terror in our God, but also mercy, kindness, redemption, and love. God seeks out his disobedient people in the garden, promises them a Savior, and, before they leave paradise, makes clothes for them (Genesis 3:9, 15, 20).

Now we learn that God longs to extend kindness to the completely undeserving. We learn that his inward bent is toward restoration—that he longs to redeem the guilty and turn them into the guiltless. We learn that he is willing to sacrifice his only Son to make our redemption possible. His grace reaches down as far as our disobedience and then goes beyond it, so we are unable to "out-sin" his redemption. If evil didn't exist, we wouldn't know the depths of God's grace and kindness.

In a world where evil did not exist, vast tracts of our Creator—the best and the most beautiful person in the universe—would be completely off limits to us. Evil, sin, and suffering create an invitation to sound the depths of our God.

Suffering Is an Invitation to Become More Like God

Suffering is also used by God to makes us more like him (Romans 8:28ff). God uses suffering to expose our hearts, to teach us to depend only on him, and to train us in faith. How does that happen?

Suffering shows us what is in our hearts. Consider what happened long ago when Moses led the people of Israel out of Egypt. They were at the edge of Canaan, the land God had promised them, but they didn't believe God was going to help them conquer the land. Because they doubted God, he allowed them to spend the next forty years wandering in the wilderness.

When the Israelites were on the verge of entering Canaan for a second time, Moses explained their wilderness suffering by telling them that God brought them into the wilderness to humble them and to reveal what was in their hearts (Deuteronomy 8:2–3). When they were hungry, would they grumble and complain? Or would they rely on God to care for them and supply their needs?

Suffering exposes our hearts in just the same way. Do we trust God, or is our hope in the good things he has given us? Suffering burns away self-deception by making us aware of what we turn to apart from Jesus to make our lives work the way we want. As we suffer, we find out if our faith in God is genuine.

It's easy to think that our faith is strong when things are going well. But it's the troubles of life that expose what's really in our hearts. Jesus explained this in the parable of the sower. When the seed (the Word of God) lands on rocky ground (our hearts) it grows quickly, but its roots are not deep. The shallow root of faith is exposed when "trouble or persecution comes because of the word" (Matthew 13:21). Then the plant of faith quickly withers and dies.

Take a moment to stop and think. What has suffering exposed about your heart?

Suffering teaches us to depend on Jesus. Centuries

later Jesus, when tempted by Satan in the same way as the Israelites (in the desert, famished after fasting forty days, and urged to provide food for himself), responded by quoting Deuteronomy 8:3: "Man does not live on bread alone but on every word that comes from the mouth of the LORD" (Matthew 4:4). He passed the test the Israelites had failed when they grumbled and complained about God.

When Jesus responded with perfect faith and perfect trust even as he suffered, he passed the test of faith not just for himself, but for all who put their faith in him. So don't be discouraged when suffering in your life exposes your unbelieving heart. Instead, confess your lack of faith to Jesus and ask him to fill you with himself. He promises to forgive you and to pour his Spirit into you so you can respond faithfully in the middle of suffering and temptation (John 14:26; Acts 2:38; 1 John 1:9).

Suffering trains us in faith. If, as we suffer, we learn to cry out to God for help and depend on him for everything, then God will use our suffering to train our faith. God did this for the Israelites as they wandered in the wilderness. When the next generation stood poised to enter Canaan, they had even more reason to doubt God's promises than their parents: Canaan was full of cities and armies that were bigger and stronger than they were forty years before, and Moses, the only leader they had ever known, wasn't going with them. Yet the Israelites responded faithfully.

They had allowed their hardships to train them in godliness (Deuteronomy 8:5; Hebrews 12:4–11). Instead of doubting God, they lived with confidence in his promises. Through many hard experiences they had found that it was true that "man does not live on bread alone but on every word that comes from the mouth of the LORD" (Deuteronomy 8:3).

How has God used suffering in your life to train you in faith? Are you learning to live by "every word that comes from the mouth of the LORD?"

Suffering trains us in holiness. When we suffer, it is easy to feel like God is punishing us. So as you think about your life and what God is doing, you need to keep in mind the very important distinction between punishment and discipline. Punishment means someone is trying to extract payment from you for what you owe them. When you think about how much debt you've racked up by sinning against an infinite God, then you quickly realize that it would take eternity to pay it off. God knows that it would be impossible for you to pay for your sins, so he sent Jesus to pay your debts. If you have put your faith in Jesus, then the pain you are experiencing has nothing to do with paying what you owe—Jesus' death paid it all. You have no outstanding debt in your relationship with God.

That's why you need to understand that what God is doing in your life is not punishment—it's corrective discipline. Those God loves do experience pain, but the pain is not punishment; it's discipline and it's meant for our good. Even verses that use the word "punish" when discussing God's people have disciplined training in view (2 Samuel 7:14–16; Lamentations 4:22). What you're experiencing is pain that is helping you grow in holiness.

But be careful! The Book of Job works hard to counteract the idea that every negative thing you experience comes because you've deserved it. Also,

When Bad Things Happen

the story of the blind man whom Jesus heals points out that his blindness was not the result of his sin or his parents' sin, but that "the work of God might be displayed in his life" (John 9:3). Every time I meditate on these passages, I become even more leery of the quick connection we often make between people's current difficulties and their previous sins.

Jesus is clear that we cannot be sure that God intends a particular suffering to connect to a particular sin in someone's life. It's wiser, therefore, to stick with what we do know: Jesus loves me and when he allows difficulties in my life, they are *always* for the purpose of drawing me closer to him and making me more like him.

Suffering Is an Invitation to Be More Involved in God's Kingdom

Suffering advances the purposes of God in the lives of his people and his kingdom. As you consider many of the people in Scripture—Joseph, David, Paul… Jesus!—you realize their sufferings benefited the larger kingdom even more than it benefited them.

Take Joseph for example. His brothers sold him into slavery and he was taken to Egypt. He suffered terribly in Egypt, yet years later he was able to feed his family during a famine because he had become a high-ranking official in the Egyptian government. When he met his brothers after many years, they worried that he would pay them back for what they did. But Joseph told his brothers not to be afraid. He said, "You intended to harm me, but God intended it for good to accomplish what is now being done, the saving of many lives" (Genesis 50:20).

All the things Joseph suffered—kidnapping, slavery, imprisonment—weren't just about making him a better man. They were to preserve the Israelites. He suffered so his family could survive. He suffered so they could find shelter in Egypt. He suffered so that years later they could become a nation. He suffered so that eventually they could have their own land. He suffered so that even later the Messiah could come, die, and rise from the dead to fulfill God's promise of a Redeemer (Genesis 3:15). He suffered so that God's people could be saved from their sins and brought into God's kingdom. In a very real way, what Joseph endured, he endured for you.

Sometimes—many times perhaps—we suffer so that others might be enriched. That's not an American view of suffering. We often blurt out, "Why me?!" as though everything that happens to us must somehow be for our own personal benefit. But the kingdom of God is bigger than any individual. You are important to God and he has a place for you in his kingdom, but he doesn't rework his kingdom plans around what you want. To do so wouldn't be best for everyone else...or for you. So you too will likely experience things you'd rather not, for the sake of bringing goodness and life to someone else.

Suffering is also a strong reminder that God's kingdom is not of this world, and this earth is not our home. When life doesn't go well, it reminds us that this earth is not paradise. Suffering helps us to consider ourselves, along with Abraham, as strangers and aliens on this earth waiting for a better home.

Why does God let bad things happen to you? That you might know him, be like him, and be a part of his kingdom going forward. That's not a full, exhaustive, completely satisfying answer…but it's not a bad start either.

Practical Strategies for Change

Since God is inviting you to a relationship, begin by talking with him about the things he's brought into your life that you don't like. If you don't know how to do that, use one of the psalms as the pattern for your conversation with God.

Start by reading Psalm 73. It is the prayer of someone who is questioning why his life has been harder than those around him. He looked around, saw wicked people doing better than he was, and complained about it. If you're feeling this way, take heart; you're in good company! God doesn't mind you asking such questions—actually he invites you to do so. He included Psalm 73 in his prayer-song book so we could use it to express our questions. But here's the rub: He doesn't promise to answer you in the way you're asking it. If you read the Book of Job, you will notice that God doesn't answer the questions Job asks. Instead, he helps Job understand that he's asking the wrong questions.

God points to himself as being supremely competent to run his world and asks, "Are you willing to trust me even when you don't like and don't understand what's happening?" (Job 38—39). Jesus was. The Father's will was to crush Jesus and Jesus trusted him, though he knew he'd be abandoned. Having put his only Son through what he did for your sake, can you trust that whatever you endure is also necessary? With Jesus promising never to abandon you, can you believe that it will not be too much for you (John 14:18; Hebrews 13:5–6)? Will you trust Jesus even if, compared to others, you are suffering unfairly?

Pray through Psalm 73 and ask God to help you say, along with the psalmist, "Whom have I in heaven but you? And earth has nothing I desire besides you. My flesh and my heart may fail, but God is the strength of my heart and my portion forever" (Psalm 73:25–26).

There are many other psalms that you could choose to express yourself to God. Psalms 10 and 55 are the heart cries of those who are bringing all of their hurts and sorrows to God. Leaf through the Psalms and find one that expresses your heart. Rewrite it to reflect your life and your experience. Make it your personal prayer to God. But don't stop there. Live out your prayer by taking a few small steps of faith toward God:

1. *Confess that God's purposes are good even when you don't fully understand them.* Sometimes this is hard to do on your own, so you may want to ask some of your friends to remind you of how they've seen God at work in you lately.

2. *Ask God to show you what is in your heart.* We can always be sure that our response to any situation reveals whether our hearts are faithful or unfaithful. Sit quietly for a few minutes, and ask God what is being revealed about what you want and long for—then either rejoice or repent…and then rejoice!

3. *Remember God's mercy to you.* Even though God tests us, he also provides for us so we're not crushed.

Can you recall some recent times in which you've seen both his testing and provision?

4. *Thank God for his mercy to you.* When was the last time you thanked Jesus for using everything in your life to draw you closer to him? When was the last time you told a friend about God's goodness to you even in your sufferings?

No one wants to suffer. People without faith in Christ see no purpose or meaning in their suffering. Without faith it seems like your suffering is the result of chaotic, impersonal forces colliding in your life with no guaranteed result. Christians, however, as they grow and reflect on their experiences are able to see the good that God brings out of it and are thankful—*not* for the suffering itself, but for him and his involvement. People regularly say, "I would never want to go through that again, but I wouldn't trade what I learned about my Lord for anything!"

Simple, Quick, Biblical

Advice on Complicated Counseling Issues
for Pastors, Counselors, and Individuals

MINIBOOK
CATEGORIES

- Personal Change
- Marriage & Parenting
- Medical & Psychiatric Issues

- Women's Issues
- Singles
- Military

USE YOURSELF | GIVE TO A FRIEND | DISPLAY IN YOUR CHURCH OR MINISTRY

New Growth Press

Go to **www.newgrowthpress.com** or call **336.378.7775** to
purchase individual minibooks or the entire collection.
Durable acrylic display stands are also available to house
the minibook collection.